The N...o...od

by Susanna Fallon

Let's walk around
the neighborhood.
Who works here?

Do you see the mailman?
This mailman brings
the mail.
What tools does he use?

Do you see the baker?
The baker makes cookies.
What tools does he use?

Is this the vet?
The vet takes care of pets.
What tools does she use?

Here is a firefighter.
A firefighter keeps you safe.
What tools does he use?

Here is a shop.
The shopkeepers sell flowers.
What tools do they use?

Let's eat some lunch!
What tools can we use?

STRATEGIES & SKILLS

Comprehension
  Strategy: Ask and Answer Questions
  Skill: Key Details

High-Frequency Words
  you

Phonics
  short *o*

Content Standards
  Social Studies
  Economics

Word count: 102**

Photography Credit: Cover Glowimages RM/age fotostock

**The total word count is based on words in the running text and headings only. Numerals and words in captions, labels, diagrams, charts, and sidebars are not included.

Education

Send all inquiries to:
McGraw-Hill Education
Two Penn Plaza
New York, New York 10121

ISBN: 978-0-02-119436-0
MHID: 0-02-119436-X

Printed in the United States.

6 7 8 9 DOC 17 16 15 14

TITLE I
Oxford Public Schools

B

The Neighborhood

by Susanna Fallon

Mc
Graw
Hill